Stand Up,
SPEAK!

**HOW TO OWN THE ROOM AS A
SPEAKER/PRESENTER BEFORE YOU BUY IT!**

JIM DINEEN

Author of
"Life's Just Not That Complicated"

Printed in the United States of America

First Printing, 2016

ISBN 978-1-945091-03-2

Ordering Information: Special discounts are available on quantity purchases by bookstores, corporations, associations, and others. For details, contact the publisher at sales@braughlerbooks.com or at 937-58-BOOKS.

For questions or comments about this book, please write to info@braughlerbooks.com.

Braughler Books
braughlerbooks.com

Contents

Content

INTRODUCTION

CENTRAL THOUGHT
Speaking and communicating is an everyday activity.
We all do it so let's be the best at what we do!

"Speak with your heart and soul first. Your mouth will then lead you to success."
Jim Dineen,
Speaker, Writer, Author

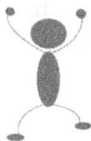

I remember being a young and rather naïve college student in the 1960's and wondering what was my reason and purpose for going to college. What was it that I wanted to be and do? I had a pretty successful cousin who was an engineer and that seemed to look rather appealing. My only problem was I was high in math aptitude and very low in math interest or application. So I dropped out of the engineering program and entered the school of business. I had a little trouble here as I knew virtually nothing about business and at the time, wasn't all that interested in business anyway. I struggled through four years of business school, working at night in a grocery store and attending class during the day. When I finally did graduate I can honestly say my biggest learning was that I was tired. What would I do with this newly earned degree and what was my goal in life? One of the best subjects I ever studied was then called public speaking. I call it my best because I realized three things;

1. I loved the class and the material.
2. I seemed to be really good at delivering the assigned material and
3. I loved the class and the material and I seemed to be really good at delivering the assigned material.

Yes, you read that correctly. The one thing I excelled at in college was "talking" and I excelled because I loved doing it! As my life and my career evolved over the next 40 years I've often gone back to that one class in school that dictated at least part of the direction my life would go. It took me many years to realize this and that is also part of the reason I am writing this book and offering what I think is sound advice. Some readers will think this is too simplistic. If you truly want to be a good speaker or presenter and you are trying to figure out what direction to go, here comes 40 years of experience.

Before I go on let me mention that in 2010 I published my first book, "Life's Just Not That Complicated". I wrote it because I believed it then and I believe it now. Life does not have to be so complicated that we don't enjoy it. Don't complicate your speaking career either. It's not that complicated if you follow this little bit of common sense.

By the fact you are still with me, you have shown a desire to start or improve your speaking skills and ability. And this ability doesn't just pertain to public or motivational or inspirational speaking. Communication seems to always be at the top of the list when analyzing issues with relationships. This concern isn't just at work or school. It is everywhere. People want to believe they know how to communicate or speak but the reality is all of us can improve. I will cover a number of areas of concern that will include presentation skills but also will examine how we can communicate better on a one on one basis as well. Becoming a speaker is not as self-explanatory as we often think. As you read through this book, continually ask yourself when, where and how can I utilize this information in my everyday life. By improving on your daily efforts to communicate more clearly and concisely, you will actually be setting the stage for a much improved career in speaking. Always remember, as YODA from Star Wars fame once said, "Do. Or do not. There is no try."

Now let's practice using our imagination. I want you to close your eyes and imagine with me for just a minute your very first speaking engagement. Now, there's at least one astute reader out there who is now saying, how do I read and close my eyes at the same time? For that one person, read this chapter and go back to using your imagination. Sometimes a speaker or a writer must be clear to be effective.

Since this is your very first professional speaking engagement and you might be just a bit nervous you don't want to worry too much. Your eyes are closed, the audience is completely quiet and their eyes are all on you. They are watching you because they have been told you will bring them the one thing they need today and you know they are right. You know that with every ounce of being in you, you are the expert in the room and these people need what you have. They need your confidence, your assurances, your knowledge, your strength, your fearlessness. They need you right now and you are going to deliver because you are the best they have ever seen or heard. You are at the top of your game and they want and need to hear that. You are (your name)------ --------- and you will deliver. You're off!

How many times in your life have you thought you wanted to be a great speaker or a great communicator? How many times have you stood in front of an audience of one or more people and quietly asked yourself, what the heck am I doing here? How often has someone so intimidated you, be it your boss, teacher, professor or maybe just a date that you simply didn't think you could speak with or respond to them intelligently? How many times have you found yourself in these situations and thought, I'd rather be dead than standing or sitting where I am? How many times have you actually realized you are perfectly normal and you fit the mold of the majority of the population? How many times have you then said to yourself; I am the best and here I come! I can do this!

A survey was taken many years ago that asked the respondents what the two greatest fears held by people in general were. When all of the answers were tallied the coordinators of the survey fully expected the number one fear held by most of us would be the fear of death and they were wrong! The survey indicated that death was the number two fear held by most of us. You've probably guessed by now that the number one fear was, is and probably always will be the fear of speaking publicly. Public speaking actually surpassed going to war and dying as the worst thing that could happen to us. I tell you this because you're normal and if speaking has got you all wrapped up in knots, fear not. You too can be fixed.

I've done a little writing in my life and it dawned on me one day how my worst critic, the person that was hardest on me and anything I put down on paper was me! How could I, the one person who was willing to take the time to spend endless hours at the computer or typewriter or with pencil and paper be so hard on myself when I didn't even have to face those who might read my writings? What was it that scared me to a point of wanting to quit? What was it that I was so afraid of? The answer was of course one that has confronted all of us at one time or another. None of us wants anything to do with rejection. Even when we're sure we are the expert on a particular subject, it is frightening to put ourselves in a position where people might criticize us. And think about this. Writing is usually done behind closed doors where we can let our thoughts and our imaginations run wild. So what is this fear of rejection doing to us that makes speaking even worse? Down deep, we all want to be liked and accepted. We can't always admit it but, we all want to be loved and treated with respect and yes, even admired. When we put ourselves out there, when we expose who we really are we are doing two things; We're showing and telling the world that we have something to say that's so important to us that we're willing to risk complete and utter rejection. But more importantly, we're telling the world that we are among the bravest people they know. We believe what we know and say and write and speak needs to be shared and we aren't afraid to risk failure to do so. As a speaker, we must accept the fact that we are different. The first step to becoming a good speaker is to understand how unique we are. Once we get over that little hurdle, it's smooth sailing from that point forward. If you ever watched Saturday Night Live on television, you may remember a character that would talk to himself in a mirror and encourage himself to be self-confident. He would say things like I am smart, I am good, I am strong, I am unique, I am talented and by golly I like myself. If you laughed at that skit then you know who and what I'm referring to. I am suggesting that each of us needs to add just one more phrase; I have something to share that others need to hear and by golly I'm fantastic at sharing my message. And I'm the best there is at conveying this information. This is your new beginning! I am speaker, hear me roar!

Let's try this one more time now. Close your eyes and imagine that you've just given a phenomenal speech on your subject. You don't see them but you can hear the audience applauding and cheering and you hear words like fantastic, wonderful, insightful and more! You feel people shaking your hand and congratulating you and thanking you. You are a speaker and you have delivered! Never ever forget this moment. It belongs to you and you alone.

I

WHAT BENEFITS WILL YOU RECEIVE FROM READING THIS BOOK?

WHY THIS BOOK AND FOLLOWING THESE STEPS WILL MAKE YOU A BETTER SPEAKER/PRESENTER

CENTRAL THOUGHT
What they will do for you and why these eight steps
will help you become a better communicator/speaker

"It is never too late to be what you might have been."

Mary Ann Evans (George Eliot)
1819-1880, Novelist and Journalist

I have always been a pretty self-confident person. I've never been so self-assured that I thought I knew everything but, I have trusted my instincts implicitly in most situations. When I read a book or newspaper or article in any format, I must first think and believe it will benefit me in some way. I need to learn or understand something more clearly or I won't spend my valuable time on reading. For that reason, I offer you these reasons to stay with this material.

- You will understand the importance of listening skills to you and your audience
- You will see how to think more clearly on your feet
- You will learn how to react to various situations and comments more clearly and effectively
- You will increase your self-confidence
- You will understand how to project more believability in your ideas and thoughts
- You will understand what is the best use of visual aids in your presentations and their importance or lack thereof
- You will learn how to organize a presentation and structure your talk
- You will recognize just how powerful you really are.

I graduated from Miami University of Ohio in 1968 and for the third time in my life, attempted to enlist in the United States Army. If you know anything about history you will recall that the mid to late 60's were no time to enlist in the military. Viet Nam was really ramping up and because I had failed the military physical before, assumed I would do so again and my wife and I could get on with life. Planning for the future was a bit challenging in those days so off I went to my local enlistment center and just as I had before, I failed the physical. The third time, at least in my estimation would be the charm. I had been married for almost three years by then, had now failed the military physical three times, had graduated from college and was ready to plan and lead my happy life. I was ready for success. I became a salesman for a national consumer products company and became pretty successful for a guy just 22 years old. I was promoted twice in a year and a half and was transferred to a headquarters town for a major distributor about 2 hours from my hometown. After purchasing our first home in our new community we were ready to start a family and get on with life. Seven days after finalizing the purchase of our new home, I was drafted and passed the physical. As I mentioned, planning wasn't easy in those days. My wife was six and a half months pregnant and I was stationed in Ft. Dix New Jersey for basic training. Following this, I was sent to Ft. Lewis Washington for advanced infantry training and this was followed by orders to Viet Nam. By then my daughter was born and after spending a short 4 days at home with my new family, I was off to war.

Now what does any of this have to do with being a speaker? My personal answer to this question is, everything. At the age of 23 I was embarking on a second and third life that I had neither planned for nor was I prepared. I left to a world I didn't know and returned to one that totally confused me.

If you wonder why I am telling you this story now, I want you to realize that at a very young age, I was presented with enough material to speak for years if I had chosen to do so. Regardless of your age or background, begin now to prepare your speech. You will need and value it later on.

II

KNOW YOURSELF AND YOUR WHY

CENTRAL THOUGHT
To be a good communicator one must know
the essence of who they are and why they
want to communicate effectively

"Remember, the thoughts that you think and the statements you make regarding yourself determine your mental attitude. If you have a worthwhile objective, find the one reason why you can achieve it rather than hundreds of reasons why you can't."

Napoleon Hill
1883-1970, Author of *Think and Grow Rich*

I want you to realize now that every great speaker was exactly like you at some time in their speaking career. What I have found that begins to bring out the greatness in us speakers is our recognition of who we are and how great we can be. We have a true understanding of exactly why we are a speaker and what we can accomplish as a presenter. We have a purpose.

Over the many years I've been privileged to present and speak to various audiences as well as hear many presentations, I've noticed one big difference between good and great speakers and those that were just so-so. The really good ones seem to have a solid handle on who they are and what they are about. Now, you may say that should be apparent but that's not my experience. Great speakers have a passion and an insight into themselves that jumps out as soon as they hit the stage. It's not just an appearance of confidence and strength, it's an aura of "I'm here and you are going to like me". You know when they arrive that they are the experts in their subject and they are confident they can share that expertise with the audience. When you can exude that kind of presence, you'll be a good and ultimately a great speaker.

Part of my varied career experience is to have counseled many individuals in job searches. These counselling sessions ranged from working with experienced senior executives to beginning level high school and college graduates and I've seen the same traits either obviously present or obviously missing. I decided as I helped these people they first off needed to get a handle on themselves and thus I developed a very simple exercise to help them grasp their true being, the why they want to do something. This is comprised of only two very simple questions. Here is the exercise and I want you to complete it.

On the left side of a piece of 8 ½" X 11" paper, write this question:

What are all of the things in life I do on a regular basis? As you list your answers, do not discriminate. This is not about your job, your marriage, your sports accomplishments or your ability to change car spark plugs. It is about all of these and much more. It is about your life. For example, I love to exercise. I love to lift weights, play golf, read, play with my grandkids and walk in the woods. I love to sit in the sun and feel its warmth and I love the beach. I also truly enjoy writing and speaking and cutting the grass and staring at clouds. These are just a few of the things I love to do and most of them have nothing to do with my writing or speaking as a career. They also have everything to do with who and what I am.

After you have exhausted this list, go to the right side of your sheet and write this question: *What are all of the things in life that I do that I'm really good at? Again, do not discriminate. Using my example, I'm a pretty good reader and I play kid's games quite well; at least the old fashioned kid's games. I'm a pretty good weight lifter as far as technique and I'm a reasonably good golfer. I can't swim more than 50 yards so that's probably not going to make this list. I think I'm a pretty good writer and I'm told I'm a very moving speaker and presenter and I can be very funny to some people.*

Once I have run out of things to put on these two lists, lay them side by side and begin to compare. Match up those that seem to have some commonality like, I love to play kids games and I'm pretty good at it. I love to play golf and I'm reasonably good at it. I enjoy lifting weights and I look like I know what I'm doing. I'll probably never win a weight lifting contest though but that's not what this exercise is about.

I hope you've gotten the idea by now. In order to be an effective speaker you must not only have valuable subject matter but be passionate about it. If you can put these two criteria together, you've got your subject matter, you've got your expertise, you've probably got your passion and you're on your way to being a great speaker.

Always remember, your speeches should accomplish 1 or more of these three things;

> P-solve a problem,
> F-address a fear,
> C-satisfy a curiosity.

If you can do 2 or 3 of these things, even better. Now why is this important? You may want to speak about the only thing you've ever done in life and it happens to relate to your current job or career path. You've done it for so long you've become known as somewhat of an expert at it but is it what you really want to do? Are you passionate about it? Let me tell you a true story that happened to me when I was doing some outplacement and recruiting work for a very large company that was in the middle of downsizing.

I was working with a lady who had just lost her job of over 25 years and she was not just down but depressed and very emotional. She was an engineer and had convinced herself that she knew nothing in life but the computer engineering she had been involved in for so long. As a result, she struggled terribly with her list when I assigned it. She was trapped in her own rut. My job was to help her work through what was actually all in her head, her imagination. She just didn't realize it. I took her aside and we talked about all of the things she did outside of work and it seemed she didn't do too much. I felt myself getting frustrated for her and then asked her why she didn't have many activities outside the workplace. Her answer shocked me and it puts into perspective how all of us can get trapped in our own little ruts. She didn't do too much outside work because she and her spouse were ballroom dancers and they spent almost all of their free time either dancing in contests or shows or teaching others to ballroom dance. She loved dancing so much and spent so much of her off time doing what she loved that she couldn't even understand it was her passion. She equated this passion to a hobby and didn't realize how really good she was.

Now, she didn't want to speak about ballroom dancing per se but she began to consider how to make a living doing things that related to her passion, dancing. Ultimately she started her own teaching academy and the last I saw of her she said she was happier than she had ever been and was making more money than as an engineer. And she was happy and fulfilled. All of us have such a passion somewhere inside of us. The exercise I want you to complete will help in discovering that passion and it exists regardless of your age, status, financial position or lot in life. If you want to be a world class speaker, that's what you are looking for.

III

WHAT ABOUT SUBJECT MATTER?

CENTRAL THOUGHT

We can't simply speak about anything/everything. We need a purpose and a degree of expertise to be effective.

"When you attain the control of the internal direction of your attention, you will no longer stand in shallow water but will launch out into the deep of life."

Neville Goddard
1905-1972, Writer and Lecturer

Now that we've got at least some level of confidence built up and we think we're kind of brave, what is it we want to talk about? Based on the previous exercise, we are on our way to subject matter and expertise. If we are fortunate enough to be an Albert Einstein or a Henry Ford or a past President of the United States, this question is probably going to be fairly easy for us to answer. However, if we're somewhat normal or at least not well known in speaking circles, this question becomes more challenging. Believe it or not, we are all experts in something that nobody knows but us. We are first and foremost, ourselves. We each have individual lives with unique characteristics, livelihoods, educations, experiences and so on. We really are unique and so we should ask ourselves what is it about me that makes me different and how can that help others? How can I help solve problems with this expertise I've acquired in life? If you have completed the exercises in the previous chapter, you're on your way to answering these questions. You now have some idea of who you are, what your strengths are, what you're passionate about and what you can do with this knowledge. Never forget that we are in a learning curve of some kind every day and our "area of expertise" may constantly be changing. And that's OK!

It's time now to do your research and this can really be not only educational, but fun. If you want to have an impact on your audience, you must have a great subject that you are passionate about, that you probably know more about than most in your audience and that you can convey with conviction and feeling and emotion and confidence and, well, you get the picture. Do you feel your confidence growing? You are developing a strength that nobody else in your audience can come close to because only you have it. It is yours and you own it. All you have to do now is share it and inspire them. Always remember PFC from the previous chapter and you'll be fine.

> P-solve a problem,
> F-address a fear,
> C-satisfy a curiosity.

I wrote a story a few years back that might help put this into perspective. My story was entitled "Forts" and it was prompted by some day dreaming I was doing on how happy I was as an 8 year old boy. My particular dream that day centered on the building of a dirt fort by me and some friends and what challenges and failures and victories we all encountered during its construction. Without telling you the whole story, it transcended into a short story about life. Regardless of your age or how your life has gone, your experiences equate who and what you are. I turned this into not only a wonderful short story, but a very heart warming speech which I've given a couple of times to very good reviews. It's my story so I am the expert in its content and in its telling. It addresses many of our everyday fears about taking chances in life and winning some battles and losing others. It can satisfy a little curiosity about whether it's sometimes worthwhile to jump off the high board just to know the feeling. Again, when you know yourself and know your expertise, regardless of how mundane you might think it is, you will have found your passion, your topic matter.

My point in telling you this is that my experience as an 8 year old boy was not only interesting to many people, it conveyed many lessons. We aren't born with all of the strength needed for survival in every circumstance we encounter. We most often must develop that strength through testing resulting in success or failure. We aren't born knowledgeable in every aspect of life but we learn and we grow and suddenly, we are quite knowledgeable in some areas. We aren't admired or liked because we are always right or correct but by how we react to the challenges we face and what we make of those challenges. Our subject matter is all around us and we must discover what to do with it. Take all of this one step at a time.

Now, you may be asking; "when do I learn to speak?" Be patient. You are learning more than you think.

IV

THE IMPORTANCE OF BEING A GOOD LISTENER

CENTRAL THOUGHT

It's easy to be a talker. How do our listeners feel and react to what we say? How do we promote good listening?

"Courage doesn't always roar. Sometimes courage is the little voice at the end of the day that says, 'I'll try again tomorrow.'"

Mary Anne Radmacher
Author and Artist

I know you are probably continuing to ask yourself, when do we get to the speaking part? Again, I ask you to be patient.

I love stories. I learn so much from stories. Some are really good and some are terribly bad but each one conveys a lesson. I am very fortunate to have been raised in an old, traditional Irish Catholic family. Already there are pictures being formed in each of your heads about my family. It's because we are all groomed to have certain notions and beliefs based on someone else's experiences. As an avid gym rat I've always been told and usually witnessed that men are stronger than women. And having grown up a boy, I know that boys are tougher than girls. Some of us have pre-conceived notions about strong men and weak women until we are proven wrong. The fact of the matter is that all men aren't stronger than all women and all women aren't weak. I lifted weights with a young woman for a few months that could bench press over 200#. Some guys reading this are saying big deal I can bench press over two hundred pounds any time. Here's the big difference. The young lady I am talking about only weighed 130# herself. For her to lift what she did was quite a feat of strength. She didn't quite meet the criteria I had heard about most of my life. Now, what does this have to do with speaking? I hope you'll see that it has to do with everything we are discussing.

Let's start with a basic premise; most of us are miserable listeners. Yes, I know we think we hear all that is said or that is presented to us but the truth is that we tend to be preparing our answer or rebuttal to a conversation or presentation long before the speaker has finished. It's not that we want to argue or don't like the delivery. It usually has nothing to do with the speaker or presenter. It's just that we tend to want to state our opinion before we even know what the other point of view even is. And it doesn't usually matter what the subject is. We hear a word or a sentence or someone says something that we simply don't agree with or it addresses a philosophy we don't adhere to and off we go. We've lost the ability to listen openly and rationally and probably have started down the path of missing the whole point of what the speaker is saying. Have you ever been in a conversation where the other party is so intent on expressing their own opinion or thought back to you that suddenly they stop mid-sentence with something like-where was I going with this? Have you ever done this?

Have you ever been in a conversation where the receiver is continually stopping or interrupting you to make "their" point? Did you ever have a boss or a teacher who loved to ask questions but rarely heard your response because they had already formed their answer for you? Maybe the best example of terrible listening skills is watching a reporter or newsperson ask questions on TV. Does it ever bother you that the questioner is interrupting the interviewee every time they attempt to respond to the question? When I see this on my TV I find myself yelling at the person in the little box to shut up, let the person answer the question. I have been in this position myself countless times in my career. Having spent almost 40 years in the HR field, I was on both sides of the desk when people would interrupt me with their response to an assumed comment or question. Too often, they had no idea what I was conveying and so one or both of us was so tuned out, no communication ever occurred. One of the most common sources of marital discord centers on just this. I learned over the years to simply be quiet, let them get it off their minds and then remind them, tactfully if possible, that I had my own answer and that if they already knew the answer or had formed an opinion to please not waste my time. More times than not, they didn't even realize they were doing it.

In order to be a good communicator or speaker, it is vital that we first understand what it is to be a good and involved listener. By involved, I'm suggesting that when someone is speaking to us, it is more than their voice that is sending a message. What is their overall posture and are they looking us in the eyes or allowing their eyes to wander? What are they doing with their hands and feet? Are they pacing or are they firmly planted in place. Are their hand motions expressive or are they tied to their sides or worse, in their pockets? If you are now asking why these questions are even raised, think of how you feel and react when someone who is addressing you allows their eyes to drift away or they begin to stutter or their lips quiver. The physical movements of a speaker, whether in front of an audience of 1 or 1000 are vital to the conveyance of a message. When you are the speaker, it's even more important that you realize and recognize this. We speak with every part of our body and not just our mouths. The messages we send are not only sent in a very different manner when we aren't active but they are received accordingly. Speaking and "delivering" a message should be a tiring experience. We must be visual as well as verbal to be effective.

Let's examine how we can use the physical body to convey a message as well as the other means of delivery available to us. And don't just think of yourself as the sender of the message. Put yourself in the position of the audience and ask yourself what is it that gets and keeps your attention? That's what your audience is experiencing.

I was taught early in my career as a "grunt" infantryman the value of listening skills. I spent way too many hours doing KP; I liked to call it kitchen police, to not realize that had I listened more intently to what my Drill Sergeant was saying I wouldn't be doing kitchen police work. And when I was on KP it began to sink in that my Sergeant was helping me understand the value of listening skills. A successful speaker or presenter who doesn't help their audience listen as intently as possibly is actually putting them through KP. They get uneasy, nervous, bored, tuned out and miss the message completely. So how do you as a presenter help the audience to listen? Let's look at a few suggestions.

Don't forget that old fact we discussed, women are weaker than me, until we find out they aren't. Don't assume you know your audience. Feel them out.

I like to address an audience quietly before I start my delivery. Now, what does this mean? When I first step in front of a group or an individual, I take a few seconds to assess them. Are they comfortable, at ease, fidgety, restless, etc.? I want to know if I must get their attention and do I need to be calm or dramatic. By first addressing them silently I give them time to settle in and me time to adjust to the changed atmosphere. This by the way only takes a few seconds. I then start my verbal delivery with something to wake them and grab their attention. You will have to use your own methods but I personally use gentle humor and often it is self-deprecating humor. Remember though that you must be comfortable and successful with humor. You don't want to start flat. This may seem quite drawn out, but remember that if you don't have them with you at the beginning it is very difficult, if not impossible, to reel them back in. When I speak, I want to be in control. I feel better and my audience can see it. They are more willing to listen when they don't have to think so much. Once they are mine I begin.

Let me remind you that this takes very little time and can save you a lot of trauma later on. Help your audience listen.

V

APPEARANCE

speaking isn't just a matter of what comes out
of the speaker's mouth. Speaking is about body
language, inflection in voice, wardrobe and
much more. Appearance is a package.

"Remember, happiness doesn't depend on who you are or what you have; it depends solely on what you think."
Dale Carnegie
1888-1955, Author of *How to Win Friends and Influence People*

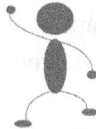

I am often asked what a good speaker looks like. My answer has always been they should look just like me. Unfortunately, most people don't want to see an old guy in sweat socks, sweat pants and a ragged old tank top. Yes, that's what I dress like at the gym. So since that answer may not fly, what should I wear and how should I appear to the audience becomes an unanswered question until now. These are the type of questions that have only one answer, it depends. It depends on what, I'm sure you're asking. Let me tell you another short story.

Many years ago I was drafted into the US Army. I was a fairly nice dresser, preppy by some standards and when I got to my first training station at Fort Dix New Jersey I looked good. At least I looked good by my standards and those of my peers back home in Ohio. Since I wasn't quite prepared for what laid in front of me I was a little shocked to find that my first Drill Sergeant didn't get as into "preppy" as I had hoped. My fellow recruits and I were immediately schooled in the art of military dress. Preppy no longer existed. From having our hair shaved completely off to being issued the ugliest green uniforms I had ever seen, we were re-educated in the proper dress attire of the military. We would soon look like everyone else around us and we began to act and be just like our fellow soldiers. Now, I'm not suggesting that a speaker should look and act just like their audience. My analogy is this; When in Rome, do as the Romans do. If your audience is a room full of business people, dress like a business person. If you are speaking to a group of children at a school function perhaps a more casual look would be appropriate. If you are a survival expert and addressing a group of survivalists, look like a survivalist. My point is to dress to meet the needs of the audience. The overwhelming majority of the time I speak I wear a sport coat and tie or a business suit. A lady may wear a business suit or dress or possibly business slacks. Remember that we are first of all trying to present ourselves as an expert or at least a knowledgeable speaker to this group of people. We are wanting to make them comfortable and at the same time, we want to be comfortable. This is a long way of saying, know your audience. Ask questions of whoever you are contracting with. Don't be bashful about asking the general background of those you will address. Are they a casual audience or a group of Drs. and nurses just coming off rounds? Have they just spent the day on a construction site or are they business people who spend their day in a nice air conditioned office. The whole idea of this short chapter is to get you thinking about the comfort and appearance and visual message you want to send. We will later cover the fact that speaking isn't all just making sound come from our mouths. You are creating an entire package when you appear in front of an audience and the better you appear to the audience the more receptive they will be. You are not just a speaker, but also a presenter so we want to "present" ourselves in the proper light. We'll talk more about this later.

Try thinking back to those days when you were looking for that first job and someone said to you, usually someone much older than yourself, "first impressions are vital to your search". It is true, you never get a second chance to make a first impression. If you show up to an interview with un-shined shoes and wrinkled clothes, un-combed hair and maybe the need for a shave or some additional makeup, people will remember one thing, your appearance. And no matter how smart you are or how well you handle yourself, what you look like is important. Speaking and speakers are no different. Regardless of your audience or your subject matter, how you first appear is important. I have learned too that asking an audience to give you permission to remove a tie or a sport coat or for a lady a sweater or jacket can serve as an opportunity to bond with the audience. Regardless of who the audience is, we all want to be comfortable. Make sure long before the actual speaking engagement that you speak with someone in the organization and ask what the normal dress code is for the group. I do this not because it will prompt some sort of dress for myself, but it sends a message that I care and it gives me a small idea of the thinking of the group. My point in all of this is to dress appropriately for your audience. They don't need to think you're one of them but they do need to relate positively to you. It will also help to calm you and your nerves down to know that the audience sees you as an ally. Always put yourself in the place of the listener and follow your gut. Rarely will you be wrong. As a general rule, always dress UP when you speak but wear attire that will enable you to be comfortable in any setting.

VI

VENUE

**WHERE WILL YOU SPEAK? • SIZE OF ROOM
NUMBER IN AUDIENCE • BACKGROUND OF AUDIENCE
LAYOUT OF ROOM**

CENTRAL THOUGHT
When presenting on any subject, utilization
of the room, its contents, the audience, the
geography of the space etc. is vital for success.

---

*"I believe life is a series of near misses. A lot of what we ascribe
to luck is not luck at all. It's seizing the day and accepting
responsibility for your future. It's seeing what other people
don't see. And pursuing that vision."*
Howard Schultz
Chairman and CEO of Starbucks

Once you have a speaking engagement, it is vital that you
know the audience, the sponsor, the venue, the size of the
room and the available props if necessary. If it seems we
are spending a lot of time on preparation, there is a reason.

Until you are a very qualified speaker and presenter, it is important that you enter a room and be in command. That doesn't mean you're arrogant or too sure of yourself, but it does mean you are as prepared as you can be for all possibilities.

A few years ago I was invited to speak to a very small group, about 25-30 nurses and technicians in a hospital setting concerning a serious topic on health. I was considered to be pretty knowledgeable on the subject and the audience was technically much more knowledgeable than was I. However, I needed to impress them with this presentation as it could lead to a very lucrative long term arrangement. I should add that this engagement required me to drive 5 hours the night before to get to my destination. I arrived about 45 minutes early to the venue and asked to see the room we would be in. To my shock I found that my original presentation room was no longer available and we would be working in a room designed for meetings of no more than 10-15 people. There was only one door at the back of the room and I would be in the front. I could barely turn around in the room and had I not scouted this issue out beforehand, it would have been a disaster. I don't like surprises as they sometimes jump up and bite me and you should handle your speaking the same way. I immediately decided against my power point presentation and got permission to make enough copies of my presentation to give each participant the pages I wanted them to keep. My presentation went great and they were appreciative of the information I left with them and yes, I got the long term commitment I was hoping for. My point is this. Your presentation will be very dependent on how you present yourself and part of that is knowing who, what, where and why you're there to begin with. Don't leave anything to guesswork. It is "always" possible to take a quick walk around a room before speaking. Get a feel for what the room is like, how big it is and where there may be little props you can use. I have gone into large venues, the night before if possible, and placed props to use during my talks. These are not gag type props, but I make sure they serve a purpose and have some value to the audience. An audience appreciates preparation. They know you care about them and the message you are sending. How you will move depends on the layout of the room and whether it is deeper or wider. Will your voice work in the back corners of the room and do the acoustics work well for you? If not, you can adjust your presentation accordingly. I treat every room as if I were there for the first time in the dark. I want to know what it feels like. Then I'll know how strong I feel.

If these suggestions seem like overkill to you I want to offer another story that actually happened to me. I had been invited to speak before a large group, approximately 700 people in New York City. Now this wasn't just any audience. These people were from throughout Europe and were financial executives. Among all of their other duties as Managers, in their respective organizations, they were also responsible for the employment function. I was presenting on career changes for people entering their organizations and what they might expect from new employees or prospective employees. I had spent over 25 years in Human Resources to include recruiting, compensation, and some counselling. I knew virtually nothing about financial issues.

As I waited my turn at the podium I realized that the speaker preceding me was at least 30 minutes over on his presentation. As I mentally covered my own presentation I was approached by the organizer of the event. He apologized profusely before asking me if I could condense my 45 minutes down to 15 and still cover all of the details desired. Panic could have set in but I had prepared. The night before, I had asked the hotel staff to allow me into the room to leave some materials. I strategically placed small booklets I had brought with me to pass out under 8-10 chairs throughout the room. I had originally planned to use these at the end of my 45 minutes. Since I felt prepared and knew where these booklets were, I quickly covered the more mundane portions of my original speech and went to what I thought was the "meat" of my topic. I did all of this in less than 10 minutes and when it came time to utilize my props, I was ready to spring into action. Over the last 5 minutes I spoke, I summarized my entire 45 minute presentation using the props or booklets as my anchors and soon received a standing ovation. My 15 minutes of fame was wonderful and led to two other presentations that year. I was given my whole 45 minutes in those presentations and they were equally well received. Preparation earned me a substantial bonus for my efforts.

VII

PREPARATION, WARM-UP, EXERCISES

CENTRAL THOUGHT

We've all been told that to exercise effectively without injury requires preparation to include warming up. Presenting is no different and that includes more than just massaging ones throat.

"The quality of a person's life is in direct proportion to their commitment to excellence, regardless of their chosen field of endeavor."

Vince Lombardi
1913-1970, Legendary Football Coach

We all have our ways of warming up for any kind of exercise. Sometimes our warm ups are in our head and sometimes we work better with a little physical movement. I am an avid exerciser and do at least an hour and a half of physical work-out every day so doing physical warm ups before a speech are already a part of my daily routine. What I realize is that I need to get my head into the task and so I've developed my own little ritual. I emphasize that this is not about my ego or my great impression of myself although self-esteem is important. I begin every pre-speech with this little sermon to myself.

"It's not easy being me! It's not easy standing up in front of all of these people as they expect great things from me, but I am up to it because I am here to dazzle them. They are paying me with their time, money, interest and desire to learn from me and I owe them. Because it is my speech, my topic, my area of expertise and soon to be my room, I am great and they will know that soon. I'm big, strong, good looking, intelligent and knowledgeable. I'm very likeable and I know how to connect. This audience is going to love me. I know it and they will soon know it. They will sell me to my next audience based on my presentation, delivery and knowledge that I am great. I own this room.

Now, I know some of this must sound like a sales job for a new car and in a sense it is. The important thing and big difference is, I am the car. I don't necessarily have to believe all of that self-talk on a daily basis but in the moments before I speak, I believe every word of it. This is my way of walking out in front of an audience with my head held high, my shoulders back, my posture as good as I can get it and most importantly to my audience, a look of great confidence and knowledge. I want them to know I'm there to make them love me. I can go back to being plain old me when I'm finished.

I have known speakers whose ritual includes jogging in place and just like many athletes, some speakers don't want anyone around them at all before starting. I have a friend who keeps a small rubber ball in his pocket and squeezes it continually to relax before he goes before an audience. He says it releases his pent up energy. If given the chance, I have another friend who simply sits in the back of the room while others before her present. She says this relaxes her and tells her the mood of the room before she goes out. What you choose to do is of course up to you. Remember, whatever works is what works for you.

In summary, make sure you know your material, know your audience, know your room, know your goal or desired end result and relax yourself physically. If you do your homework and you warm up properly, you can't fail. One of my favorite sayings comes from the movie Star Wars. YODA said, "Do, or do not. There is no try". Let this be your mantra and you will dazzle any audience.

VIII

EYE CONTACT / OWNING THE AUDIENCE

CENTRAL THOUGHT

The most important tool used in any presentation may not be the voice, the dress, the layout of the room or a myriad of other items. Effective use of the eyes can make or break a presentation.

"The start is what stops most people."

Don Shula
Former NFL Coach

I am a Viet Nam Infantry Veteran and very proud of it. I'm a husband of 50 years, father of 2 beautiful daughters, grandfather of 5 and I've had a few experiences in life.

I'm a business owner, employee, entrepreneur, with successes and failures and I'm still walking upright.

I'm a man with some health issues. I deal every day with kidney disease and a transplant, liver disease, a touch of asthma and the beginnings of arthritis. I have a hard time seeing without my glasses and I visit a cancer doctor every three months to have some more stuff frozen, cut, burned or creamed off.

I'm an avid exerciser. I'm a weight lifter who at 70 years can still bench press 150#, curl 35# and follow all that with a brisk 10 minute mile. I'm you in 10, 20 or 50 years or so and nothing I can do today will change what I've been in the past.

I am a speaker, a presenter, a performer and an inspirational motivator. I want my audience to know me and feel who I am. When I tell a story I want my listeners to be there with me and so should you. I have found that there are two proven techniques or approaches to connecting with the audience. Both are simple and require no special talent. They do take a little courage but if you've done all of your preparation properly, they will work.

First, develop a connection with your audience. As I stated in the first part of this chapter, tell them who you are but do it in a different manner than the usual introduction. Give them snippets of you, your life, your family, your geography, your story. That doesn't mean tell them your topic or your speech and it doesn't mean doing what I just did in the first section of this chapter. Tease them with what an interesting and exciting speaker they are about to hear. You can see from my first paragraph that in a few simple statements you can get them interested in you long before you get them interested in the topic. Ask yourself what it is that you do when you meet someone for the first time. Do you ask questions about them and they in turn ask questions pertaining to you? The more we get to know a person the more we like or maybe dislike them. Since your audience can't ask you questions, at least not yet, give them something to intrigue them. Make them want to know more. Let me give you an example.

I wrote a story a few years ago based on a true story that happened to me as a boy. The story was titled "The Fort" and it concerned a rock and dirt fort that was built when I was 8 years old with a group of friends. The story had a moral to it and it covered the learnings of a group of 8 year old boys on one beautiful sunny afternoon in July in Southern Ohio near the Miami River. That's all the information I'm going to give you. Does it make you think? Do you wonder just what the story was about or how it turned out? I introduced a speech I gave many years later with just about that much information and the speech was titled "Growing Wise". It lasted about 45 minutes and my audience totaled about 300 participants. I had them on the edge of their seats for the entire time because each and every one of them could relate immediately to me. Everyone who is an adult has been 8 years old at some time. Everyone in that audience has seen a big beautiful body of water somewhere in their life and most if not all know where Southern Ohio is. My point is that I had them with me before I told them anything about growing wise. You have such stories and it's important that you master your stories in very brief form. Learn to tease. This technique will not only help you capture the audience, but you'll hold their attention because you are the expert on the subject and nobody can refute what you're saying. You are the only one in the room who has had that particular experience. You own the listeners.

The second technique I use every day of my life is eye contact. It's amazing how in control of any situation you can be by simply using eye contact.

Now this can be a rather frightening experience but used properly can make you a powerful communicator. When I was first beginning my speaking career and long before I knew what I was doing, I received some of the best advice I've ever gotten. A very experienced presenter that I met was evaluating my speaking and presenting skills. He was not a public speaker, but a gentleman I met while we both participated in a class. We had coffee together and lunch together for three days in a row. He watched as I struggled with presenting topics to older more experienced speakers, some of whom were my bosses. He asked me how I felt when I talked with him or any other person one on one. I answered that I loved to communicate with people and had developed the habit of not just listening to the other party but watching them as well. I explained that it was very comfortable for me to speak with people I knew, as well as strangers, as I felt in control of myself. When asked if I felt in control of the listener in an audience of more than one I said of course not and this is where he helped me develop a lifelong love of communicating. He reminded me that when I spoke to people, one on one, I had a great habit of looking them in the eye. I told him my father had always told me to look a man in the eye when talking with him and I felt good doing so. He then asked why I didn't do the same with an audience. Why did I tend to look over the heads of the audience or at the top of their heads? Sometimes he told me I even talked to the wall in the back of the room. I explained to him that I shied away from talking to the audience because it was a bit threatening to see all of those faces staring back at me. He then asked me what the difference was between talking with the audience and with a person one on one. I didn't really understand what he meant and he explained by asking this question; What is the difference between talking to hundreds of people at once or just one person at a time? I had no answer. He told me why it was confusing for me to answer. He stated that it's because there is no difference.

He explained to me how, with a little practice, I could personally talk with countless people in an audience by addressing them one at a time for just a few seconds. This seemed rather strange to me but I began following his advice and it worked. I found that when I moved my eyes around the room and found a different face every couple of seconds I could speak directly to every member of the audience and give them the personal feeling of me talking only to them. The more I practiced the better I got at it. Today people compliment me on speaking directly to them during a speech or meeting. I am what's called a Lector at my church where I read the word of God to the congregation. Regardless of the length of the reading I have found that by moving my eyes around the body of the church and addressing as many faces as possible, people feel that I'm talking to them.

As a presenter, we have two basic options, that if used well, will always be beneficial to us. Visual and vocal control can make or break a good presentation. I'll say a little more about visual aids soon, but for now, know that if you can control your eye contact, your visual delivery will be very strong. When you use various inflections or volumes or pronunciations you are adding to that strong delivery. Learning to interact with an audience for me is like weight lifting or golf. The more I practice the better I become.

So in summary, use your eyes to help control the situation and preface this by creating a bond or relationship with the audience. Make them your friend and tease them with just enough information to make them want more. Practice these two habits and your speaking prowess will grow tremendously.

IX

THE FIRST SIXTY SECONDS UP FRONT, FIRST ACTIONS ON STAGE

CENTRAL THOUGHT
A successful speaker or presenter must
have their own style, their own method
of taking control of the audience.

"When in doubt, make a fool of yourself. There is a microscopically thin line between being brilliantly creative and acting like the most gigantic idiot on earth. So what the hell, leap."

Cynthia Heimel
Playwright, Television Writer, and Author

You've done all of your homework. You know your subject. You've studied your audience. You're familiar with your room and you've done your warm ups. You are ready! Or are you?

All of the work you've done to this point is for naught if you, as the Cowardly Lion in the Wizard of Oz would say, ain't got no courage. Early in my speaking career I realized how frightening it can be when you first walk out in front of a group, regardless of the size. I began watching other speakers to try and understand how they handled those first few seconds. I saw two things that the great presenters did that the bad ones did not.

I was privileged to see the great Zig Zigler a couple of times in person and he had a style that I soon realized I couldn't emulate. Even in his later years he had more energy than ten speakers. He would bound onto a stage and never slowed down until he was finished. Now I have a lot of energy but nothing to match his.

I also noticed many of the great speakers began quite differently but just as effectively. The Rev. Billy Graham and Bishop Sheen were always two of my favorites as their method of grabbing attention was more my style. Even setting aside that their message was more of a religious nature than that of Zig Zigler, their style was very effective at getting audience attention. Each, in their own way, would address the audience either quietly, sometimes without any sound at all, or they would calmly draw the audience to them. By the time they began to speak the listeners were straining to hear them speak. I liked this style and began to practice it for myself.

So what I'm suggesting to you is first and foremost, your style must be your style. If you are a Zig Zigler type, full of energy and can maintain a high degree of energy then by all means go for it. If you're like me, a calmer approach may be more appropriate. When I begin any speech, I calmly walk across the stage, surveying the audience as I pace. I look for familiar faces, friendly faces that I can use during my presentation. Sometimes, those faces are just to reassure myself that this is a friendly group. I "eyeball" the entire room to see what may be going on that I'm not aware of and I refresh my previous trip around the room, see chapter 6, so I have those familiar markers. You may be thinking by now that the audience is falling asleep but just the opposite is happening. They are anticipating what is coming next and I'm now relaxed enough to deliver my opening. I face the group and begin. All of this takes less than 20 seconds and two very important things are accomplished.

I am now quite relaxed and ready to work. They are ready to see if I can deliver.

X

VISUAL AIDS AND FACTUAL INFORMATION

CENTRAL THOUGHT

If you've ever tried to lose weight, you know that a cardinal rule is too much of anything is unhealthy. The same is true with a good presentation.

"It isn't necessary to see a good tackle...

You can hear it."
Knute Rockne / Notre Dame

I will have very few words on this subject as I find it to be a crutch for a boring presentation. Now don't get me wrong. There are many presentations, especially in an educational or business context that need hard facts and pictures. Even in the form of numbers and graphs these can be beneficial. To make my point though, let me ask you a question.

Have you ever been to a presentation/speech where the speaker has endless power point slides or even flip chart paper that are so filled with data that even Albert Einstein couldn't read or interpret them? And when this happened, were you ever bored to tears or worse? Was it a relief when the presentation was finished and did you remember all of that data? Hopefully, I'm making a point here.

Just like eating a 10 course meal will be very unpleasant if it's all consumed at once, so does the human brain get too filled with data to the point that mental indigestion quickly sets in. As a presenter, we want our audience to remember what we've dished out and we want them to digest the content. Too many slides, flip charts and power point pieces of data too often get in the way. Feed your audience small bites of information and they will better digest the meal. There's nothing wrong with visual aids. Just don't choke your audience with so much written data that they consume none of it. Remember, spoon feeding is much better on the digestive tract, both physical and mental than eating with a shovel. I treat all of my audiences with as much gentleness and consideration as possible. I'm not suggesting you treat them as if they were ignorant but realize that an audience is made up of many different individuals. The attention span and retention capability of the entire audience must be considered. Impact is the key word, not volume. Always remember, if you must use slides or power point or flip charts use as few words or visuals as possible and more slides or charts. An audience will appreciate it.

XI

CLOSE, LEAVE THEM WITH A MESSAGE

CENTRAL THOUGHT

Have you ever gotten a song so stuck in your head
you can't quit singing or humming it? That is what
you want with your presentation. The audience
should not be able to get it out of their head.

*"I shall pass through this world but once. Any good, therefore,
that I can do or any kindness that I can show to any fellow
creature, let me do it now. Let me not defer or neglect it for I
shall not pass this way again."*

Stephen Grellet
1773-1855, Missionary

There's an old saying in the storytelling business that goes
something like this: Tell what you're going to tell them, tell
them, tell them what you told them. The point to remember

here is this. You want people to remember what they came to hear. We want our audience to remember the message but we also want them to think about the presenter. As a successful speaker, we want to be like a guest for dinner. We want to make a good enough presentation to be invited back or at least to be invited to another venue. I have found after countless presentations, meetings, and discussions that people tend to remember what impacts them personally. We all have a little selfish side. My favorite ending takes the audience back to the beginning. I remind them of where we've been, what we discussed or heard and finally, what we will do with the information.

I like to leave them with a question.

Let me give you an example.

I have been very fortunate and quite blessed to have survived a number of life threatening situations in my life. I don't think I have any cat in my heritage but I have gone through a few lives. I made it through a serious car wreck when I was a young man where I was partially scalped. I always seemed to be one step ahead of tragedy when I served in Viet Nam. Later in life I dealt with and won, at least as well as I could win my battle with kidney disease, dialysis and transplant. When I am addressing a group on any health related topic, I find it very effective to end with a question concerning what would the audience do if they were confronted with one or more of my trials. How do they think they would react or handle a life threatening or life altering situation. I know that some of them have been in similar situations and if they have, they can more readily relate to me. If they have not, I want them to remember the challenges I've experienced and how I came through them.

If I'm speaking on a particular business subject, I will have reminded them of my time in the corporate world and its challenges. I would cover what it was like to start and successfully manage my own business and yes, what it was like to lose it all due to my illness. I would then ask them what they would have done in a similar situation.

My purpose in leaving them with a question that relates to them personally and in relation to me and my life experience is to keep them involved. If I have done my job as a speaker, they are already somewhat if not completely in my corner. As they leave my presentation, I want them to feel that they can relate to all they've just heard and act on it. I will often ask them to write down my question and answer it later when they have had time to think it through. Remember, we want to be invited back to the table. Only good friends invite us back and that's what I want to be remembered as, a good friend who had something great to say. I want to be remembered!

XII

QUESTION AND ANSWER CONTROLS

CENTRAL THOUGHT

You began your speech by taking control of the room and the audience. Don't lose control just because you think you're finished. You are not finished until you leave the building.

One of the biggest mistakes a speaker can make at the end of a presentation is to ask the audience if there are any questions. This actually surprises many new speakers but it is because it can create the most difficult situation of the entire speech. What if nobody responds? There becomes a terrible silent void and it is very difficult to get out of such a situation.

I personally like to end my presentations with a question of my own to the audience. The entire purpose at this point is to gage the audience reaction to the presentation and to create a dialogue. It is great when a question causes an overwhelming response, but what if it does not. I know this may sound like cheating, but I am very careful to close on as positive a note as possible. I always make sure that someone in the audience is on my side and I give them the answer beforehand. However, I give them the answer in the form of a discussion enhancer, not a yes or no response. I want to create a situation where the audience is forced to think about what they have heard and, remember, leave with some questions about how they will use the information just received. If there are a couple of people in the audience that I know can do this, I create a question for each of them. The audience doesn't know I've done this and it enhances my final remarks in a positive light.

Another possible close or wrap up is to ask the audience to think of a circumstance that matches what I've just spoken about. Ask how they would have handled it. Ask if they are willing to share their answer and then start a conversation among all members around the workability of the answer. However you engage the audience, remember that the goal is to keep them thinking of what you've just presented. Offer them your email address to contact you with any questions or comments. Always make sure you respond to such emails.

My whole point of a good, sound closing is to create awareness of what they have heard and to encourage them to act on their feelings. We always want them to remember us, our topic and what actions will result from the presentation. If we accomplish that, we are a polished speaker. Keep them thinking and you will have succeeded!

SYNOPSIS

"Any of us can be or do anything if we want to do it badly enough. Remember, there never was and never will be another you. Don't waste you!"

Jim Dineen
Author, Speaker, Writer, Survivor

Any speech or presentation is a reflection of the speaker or presenter. The person in the speaker's chair is the boss, the manager, the person in control, the expert on the subject, the leader of the group. If that person isn't completely and totally prepared for all contingencies, they have not done their homework or more importantly, done their homework well. There is more to speaking than just "flapping your jaw". It takes work to be a good speaker or presenter and one must educate themselves on all of the big and little techniques of presenting. A speaker is a talker, a listener, an actor, a model, a friend and a critic. A speaker is all of this and more. As a young boy I learned one of the greatest lessons in my life as a Boy Scout. It doesn't pertain to just boys but to all persons in all walks of life. "Be Prepared!"